Fielding Postcard

by Ray Newton

Colour scenes from the early 1900s of London's East End published by newsagent Charles Fielding

History of Wapping Trust

Book compiled by Amanda Day, Helen Keep and John Tarby
Photography and design by John Tarby FRPS

Published by The History of Wapping Trust
1 Green Bank, Wapping, London E1W 2PA
Registered Charity No. 290087

ISBN: 978-1-873086-08-7

Printed on FSC-certified paper by Angel Press, London

Design © History of Wapping Trust 2025   Photography © John Tarby 2025

Acknowledgements

Ray Newton for postcard collection

Steve Kentfield for postcard collection

Phil Mernick for postcard collection

> **Ray, Steve and Phil's passion for collecting and sharing their postcards has made this book possible**

Ray Newton for original text from *Postcard of the Month*

Amanda Day for supplementary postcard text

Helen Keep for proofreading and subsequent research, writing and text editing

Rose Fenn for supplementary proofreading

John Tarby for all photography, typesetting, design and layout

Kevin Fernandes at Aldgate Press for postcard reproduction tests

Steve Sorba from Angel Press for managing printing and binding

References:

Tower Hamlets Local History Library & Archives

Dr Ruth Slatter, University of London

Professor Brad Beaven FRHistS, University of Portsmouth

Revd. Peter McGeary, St Mary's Church, Cable Street, Shadwell, London

Table of Contents

Page	
3	Table of Contents
4	Foreword by Steve Kentfield
5	Introduction
6	In Memory—Raymond Victor Newton
8	Watney Street E.
10	Watney Street E. (reverse)
12	Watney Market, Commercial Road End
14	Christ Church, Watney Street
16	Christ Church (interior). Watney St.
18	St. Mary's & St. Michael's Church
20	St. Mary's & St. Michael's Church (interior)
22	St. Paul's Shadwell
24	People's Palace, Mile End Road
26	Stepney Church
28	Ratcliff Highway
30	St. George's Library & Town Hall
32	St. Mary's Shadwell
34	St. George's Wesleyan Chapel
36	Interior St. George's Wesleyan Chapel. Cable St. E
38	London Docks Entrance, Leman Street
40	Interior London Docks. From Wapping Bridge
42	St. Peter's London Docks
44	St. Peter's London Docks. E
46	St. John's Schools, Wapping
48	Children's Hospital. St. George's
50	St. George's Church
52	St George's Recreation Ground
54	St. George's Church From Grounds
56	Wapping Fire Station
58	Wapping Bridge, Showing Wapping Church
60	Tunnel Pier, L.C.C.
62	The Sailors' Home, Well St. & Dock St.
64	Pier Head. Wapping
66	The Jetty London Docks
68	Dockers' Cottages. Pennington St. E
70	Whitechapel Library & Art Gallery
72	Stepney Temple. Commercial Rd. E
74	Swedish Lutheran Church Princess Sq.
76	Index of Postcard Captions by Topic
77	About the Author
78	Our Production Process

Foreword by Steve Kentfield

Picture postcard collecting saw a revival in the mid-1970s and I became a serious collector of these postcards in the early 1980s. I discovered views of the East End that were (then) nearly 100 years old. They revealed considerable physical change from the effects of World War Two bombing and post-war redevelopments. Living in Wapping at the time, I soon realised how scarce and unique some of the views I was discovering were.

There were plenty of opportunities to source postcards in those days — from markets, fairs and shops — and, in my opinion, I soon had quite a unique collection. To me, postcards became the evidence of the past, especially of where I lived, and so began my interest in local history and I met Ray Newton for the first time.

Ray was running a Local History evening class at the local institute at Broad Street School on The Highway in Wapping. My father attended the class before I did and he often spoke of my collection to Ray and other classmates, saying that I wouldn't let the postcards out of my sight to anyone. However, when I later joined Ray's class, I was happy to show them off to the delight of all!

Ray was quick to want to be involved with postcard collecting as well, seeing their potential as evidence in local history lectures and talks. We soon teamed up to hunt down postcards at shows all over the country. Our focus was on London, particularly East End London, but other topics also interested us.

Ray and I often went to the pub after the class and one day after chatting to his cousin, Tom Newton, Ray encouraged me to publish some of my postcards in a book. I was happy to do that as a collaboration with the History of Wapping Trust of which we were all members. Thus, Ray and I published our first picture postcard volume *A Riverside Journey* in 1990. The book presented postcards in black and white covering Tower Bridge to Blackwall Pier over the period 1900-1930s.

The appreciation of what I had collected by then became more apparent with the book's publication. That appreciation continues today, thanks to Ray and the History of Wapping Trust.

We always aimed to produce another postcard book and the idea for this one began many years ago. We admired the colour and quality of Fielding's postcards showing our East End. But we always felt that we didn't have enough material or knowledge of the publisher himself. Years on, little has changed with the knowledge but with the sad demise of Ray in 2024, it seemed important to publish this volume in his memory as a lasting tribute to his energy and enthusiasm for the subject matter.

Picture postcards like those of Fielding always bring back so many memories when they are viewed. To me, however, the memories of discovering them with Ray stands out most of all.

I hope you enjoy them too.

Introduction

The *Fielding Postcards* story begins in Edwardian times when postcards were in their 'heyday' – when a postcard was used as a short note to send to family, acquaintances or businesses. This was at a time when most people did not have cameras, let alone telephones and email.
A postcard was viewed as a cheap and effective means of communication and demand for them was high. The Edwardian period was known as the 'Golden Age' of picture postcards and in the peak years of 1906-1915, up to 900 million postcards were posted. Collecting postcards also became a worldwide, fashionable craze, with families filling albums which took pride of place in their homes. Businesses quickly established themselves as postcard publishers to feed that craze.

Charles Aland Fielding picked up on this craze and started publishing local scenes of Wapping and Shadwell, selling these beautiful colour postcards from his newsagent and tobacconist shop at 86 Watney Street in East London. Watney Street at the time ran from Cable Street in the south up to Commercial Road in the north. It was a bustling, noisy, vibrant street full of shops and market stalls.

Fielding's postcard production appears to have begun about 1905 and lasted possibly until the World War One period, judging by the postally-used examples we see today. Many postcards at the time were printed in Germany, where the best printing processes were available. Sadly, the outbreak of World War One in 1914 put a stop to this and production of postcards largely ceased. After the war, the General Post Office also increased the cost of sending postcards and this added to the demise of the collecting craze. Many fine printing houses then turned their attention to other publications or disappeared altogether.

When Charles Fielding died in 1920, his youngest son, Harold, carried on the newsagent business. No postcards appear to have been produced after that time.

The postcards we have reproduced in our book open a small but important window onto times past. Many of the buildings are still visible today, but sadly many are not and some of the scenes provide the only visual record of the East End's rich industrial and cultural past.

In Memory

Raymond Victor Newton

3 March 1938 — 30 April 2024

Teacher
Local Historian
Gardener
Collector of Postcards

Watney Street E.

This postcard is a view of the Fielding newsagent shop in Watney Street from where the collection of colour postcards in this book was published.

Family ancestry research has revealed the following about Fielding:

Charles Aland Fielding was born in Chippenham, Wiltshire in January 1858 to Henry Fielding and Charlotte Jane Aland. Charles lived in Chippenham and then Llanelly, formally Breconshire. In December 1877, aged almost 20, he married Sarah Ann Allaway from Bradford. The marriage took place in Lambeth, London and Charles lived in London, specifically Deptford, until at least 1911. He died in Kent on 30 July 1920, aged 62.

According to the 1911 Census of England and Wales, Charles and Sarah had seven children of which four were surviving in that year. Edward was their first born in 1879, with Ethel Allaway second in 1882. Their youngest son was Harold, born in 1890. Ethel and Harold were living with their parents in Deptford at the time of the Census.

Charles opened his newsagent and tobacconist shop *C.A. Fielding* at 86 Watney Street in 1870. He was known to supply newspapers to St. George's Library.

Charles also had a china and glass shop at 82 Watney Street and another tobacconist shop at 30 King David Lane, Shadwell.

When Charles died, Harold took over his father's business at 86 Watney Street.

The premises were very close to Shadwell station on the East London railway line. This would have allowed an easy 'commute' for the family and also a high footfall of market shoppers.

Dear Harry
    Dad has had some local views taken I thought you would like one of the shop. Hope you are enjoying yourself.   Yours sincerely
        E. Fielding

Lance Corporal Spratt
M. Company
2nd 2.O.R.W.K. Regt
West Kent Volunteer
Brigade Camp
Arundel
Sussex

Watney Street E. (reverse)

Greetings from 'E. Fielding' to a soldier

This postcard is the reverse side of the previous view of the Fielding shop. We do not know which child of Charles Fielding is writing to the soldier. The 'E' could be Edward, aged 26 or Ethel, aged 23, at the time. The postcard is franked 2.15pm on 11 August 1905 and shows what is described as a 'divided back'.

Royal Mail allowed divided back postcards in 1902, enabling both the message and the address to be written on the back of the card. A vertical line separated the message (on the left) from the address (on the right). Previously, the entire back of the postcard was used for the address and any message had to be written on the space beside the picture on the front. This was called an undivided back — see the Children's Hospital. St. George's postcard as an example.

This change from 1902 onwards led to a significant increase in the popularity of picture postcards, as the entire front could now be used for a full-size illustration.

With postcard collecting now a craze, we believe Charles seized a business opportunity to sell postcards in his shop. An enterprising man in his 40s, combined with local or itinerant photographers taking local scenes, and the availability of printing in Germany, produced a unique product—a colour postcard—that Charles could display and sell in his shop.

In 1906, the divided back format was universally accepted worldwide through the Universal Postal Union (UPU).

The view above is a transcription of the handwriting in the same layout but in a more legible form and typeface.

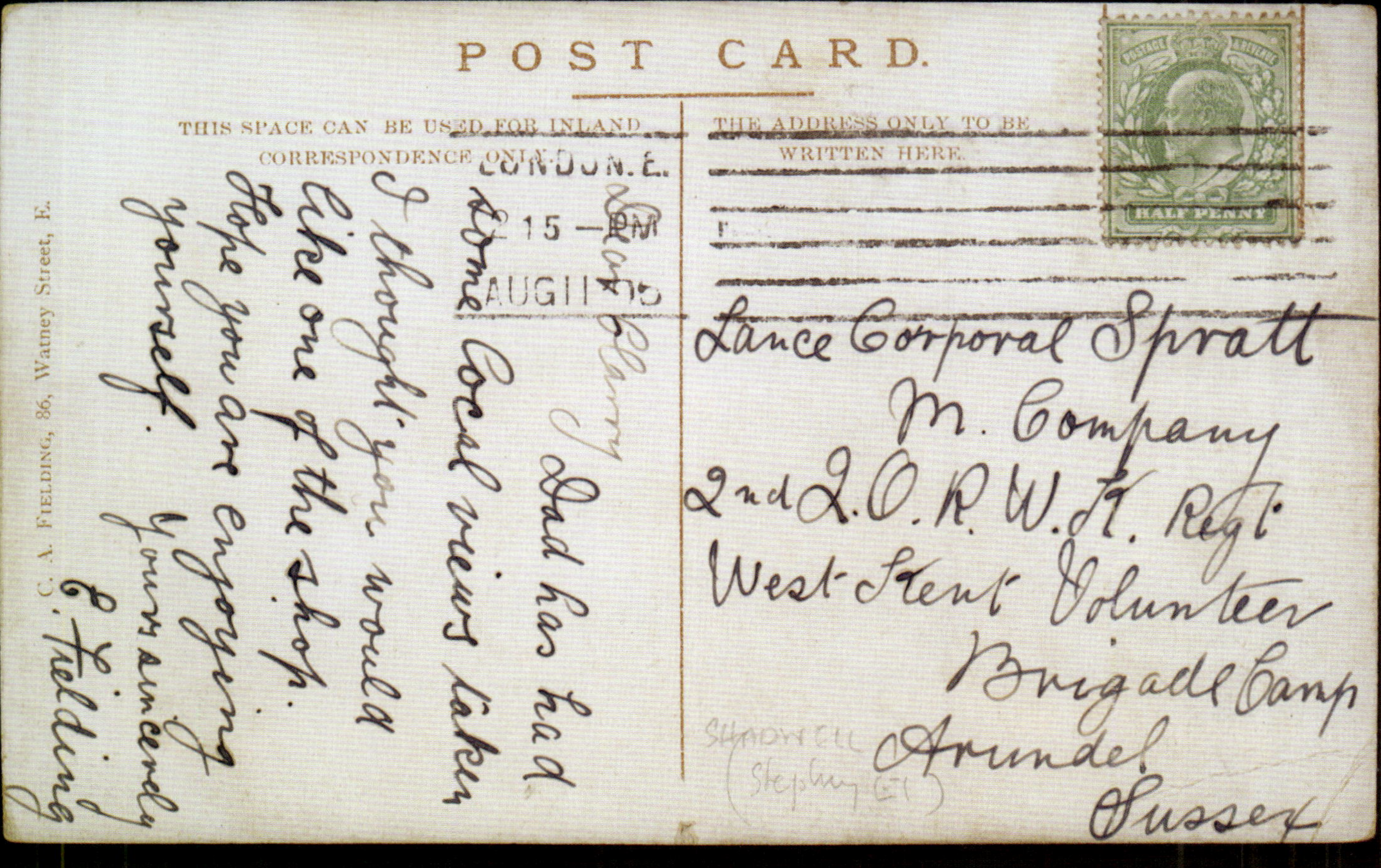

POST CARD.

THIS SPACE CAN BE USED FOR INLAND CORRESPONDENCE ONLY.   THE ADDRESS ONLY TO BE WRITTEN HERE.

C. A. Fielding, 86, Watney Street, E.

Dear Harry
Dad has had
some local views taken
I thought you would
like one of the shop.
Hope you are enjoying
yourself.
Yours sincerely
E. Fielding

Lance Corporal Spratt
M. Company
2nd 2.O.R.W.K. Regt
West Kent Volunteer
Brigade Camp
Arundel
Sussex

Watney Market, Commercial Road End.

Prior to bombing raids during the Blitz which destroyed virtually everything shown in the postcard, Watney Street was a thriving, busy street where you could buy almost anything. It rivalled Petticoat Lane and was one of London's largest markets with 200 stalls and 100 shops, including an early branch of the grocer J. Sainsbury at 66-67, not far from Fielding at 86.

The shops that can be seen in the postcard, dating from around 1906, are W. Hatch & Sons (bootmakers), Solomon Harris (surplus salvage stock) and Charles Johnson (stewed eel house). There were another eight bootmakers, 12 butchers and fishmongers, a public house at 7 *The Masons Arms,* four beer retailers, a couple of dairies and cheesemongers, a tripe dresser and a corset maker.

Christ Church, which was destroyed in 1941, was next to *The Masons Arms*.

The Fielding shop opened in 1870 and was well positioned at the Cable Street end near Shadwell station. Being the only newsagent/stationer/tobacconist/fancy goods shop in the street, it certainly appears to have captured the market. However, following post-war demolition of the north end of Watney Street, a large redevelopment by the Greater London Council (GLC) was promised but not completed until 1976. By then, the Market had been more or less abandoned and many of the remaining shops were bulldozed.

At the southern end of Watney Street was the London and Blackwall Railway which had run from the City of London to the docks on the Isle of Dogs since 1840. It closed in 1923 for passengers and 1968 for freight. However, the Docklands Light Railway, which opened in 1987, used much of the line and a new Shadwell station, previously at the eastern end of Shadwell Place, opened at the Watney Street end, close to the East London line, now the Windrush line.

The contemporary photograph was taken from Tarling Street looking north, with a car park and service road for Watney Market.

WATNEY MARKET, COMMERCIAL ROAD END.

Christ Church, Watney Street.

In the 1830s, following the passing of the Ecclesiastical Commissioners Act, the Church of England agreed to a new church in the Parish of St George-in-the-East which included this part of Commercial Road. A site was found which was owned by the Mercers' Company, a City of London livery company. At that time the land was leased to a local builder, George Bridger, who gifted the lease on condition that he built the church and it was designed by architect John Shaw Jr. The site was acquired on 27 March 1839 and Christ Church was consecrated on 11 March 1841. It ran from Dean Street (now Deancross Street) to just shy of Watney Street and was bounded by *The Masons Arms* public house to the south. Later, two houses on Watney Street were bought and adapted to be the vicarage.

The first priest of Christ Church and driving force was William Quekett. The church had a large capacity and was able to accommodate 1,537 including 635 seats for the poor. Although the congregation seems huge today, Anglican church attendances in the area were already in decline and were further reduced following an influx of Jewish refugees from Europe.

Owing to the vast size of Christ Church, it became a significant landmark. However, all this came to an end on the night of 16 April 1941 when a huge landmine totally destroyed the church and surrounding area, leaving just the church walls standing. The congregation moved to St George-in-the-East on Cannon Street Road only for that church to be destroyed just one month later with only its walls remaining.

The Christ Church site was cleared in the 1950s and it took almost 20 years to be redeveloped as the pedestrianised Watney Market and Winterton House, a Greater London Council (GLC) housing estate.

The contemporary photograph shows the approximate location of the church building which is now Winterton House car park.

Christ Church (interior). Watney St,

Christ Church was built in Romanesque style, with grey bricks and stone dressing. The church's architect, John Shaw Jr, argued for it to be built in that style rather than Gothic with cast iron pillars and Norman arches.

At the west end were two towers capped with slated pyramidal spires. Between the spires was the main door to the church. Inside space was maximised by building an arcade of two tiers to accommodate the galleries. Whilst the building was paid for by a parliamentary grant, fitting out the interior was the work of the priest William Quekett, who had to raise £350 for fixtures, an organ and heating.

Additions to the interior, until the end of the 19th century, were a work in progress. A chancel was added by building into the east wall to replace the rails around the altar and the plain galleries were decorated at a cost of £1,400. The church attracted many well connected clergy from Oxford and Canterbury who were able to raise private funds for refurbishments. Thus, the interior was improved until by 1885, Christ Church had one of the finest interiors of the East End.

One month after the centenary of its consecration, enemy action in April 1941 destroyed Christ Church. The church was never re-built. The site was cleared much later to make way for housing and shops. The church's silver communion set is now in use at St George-in-the-East Church.

It is not possible to show a contemporary photograph. The view of Winterton House car park, off Deancross Street shows the site of where the church interior once was.

Christ Church (interior), Watney St.

St. Mary's & St. Michael's Church. Commercial Rd. E.

St Mary and St Michael's Church dates back to 1762 when the Virginia Chapel was opened in Virginia Street, off Ratcliff Highway, now The Highway. The chapel was destroyed during the Gordon Riots in 1780 and re-built. However, by the mid-19th century, there was a need to build a new church for the growing congregation. The Roman Catholic Church drew up plans to build it in Commercial Road.

Father James Webb, who had been appointed as the first priest at the Virginia Street Chapel, was also the last priest in England to be charged under the Penal Laws prohibiting Catholic worship. He spent almost 18 months in Newgate Prison, City of London, before his case was dropped.

During World War Two, on the afternoon of 17 March 1945, a V2 rocket fell in Lukin Street which runs along the side of the church. It destroyed the Church School in Lukin Street and the Presbytery behind the church as well as a number of houses in Lukin Street itself. Luckily, the school was empty at the time because it was a Saturday. However, four people were killed: one in the school (a London County Council employee) and three in Lukin Street. Many were also injured by flying glass in Commercial Road. St Mary and St Michael's Church, although badly damaged by the blast, was repaired and today continues to be a thriving community.

The spirit of the parish and the resilience of the East End were shown at a wedding scheduled for one o'clock on the Saturday afternoon at St Mary and St Michael's Church. After the rocket strike and with several people killed and buildings damaged or demolished, the priest, bride and groom and their guests dusted themselves off and the wedding went ahead amid the rubble of the church with only the slightest of delays.

St. Mary's & St. Michael's Church (interior) Commercial Road, E.

The Church of St Mary and St Michael was opened in 1856 and can claim to be the oldest Roman Catholic Church in the East End. Designed by W. W. Wardell and built of Kentish ragstone with Caen stone dressing, the church's interior has a long and lofty nave with the same proportions from the entrance to the chancel. It is 185 feet long and 75 feet wide. The High Altar was erected in 1911, consisting of Caen stone and elaborately carved with marble columns and dressings.

1906 was a golden jubilee year for St Mary and St Michael's Church but its realisation began many years earlier when local Catholics raised half of the £3,000 needed to buy the land freehold for the site on the newly-created Commercial Road. By the time the church opened, it had cost £30,000 funded by donations and loans.

Although a 250 foot spire was abandoned during building, a stained-glass window was installed in 1879. Stations of the Cross were also added in 1902.

Constant improvements and rebuilding of the church have continued since 1856 and have nearly always been made possible by donations from the local congregation. This was in spite of widespread poverty and Catholic priests highlighting the threats of starvation.

The Church of St Mary and St Michael was the biggest Catholic church in London when first built and in 2001 was Grade II listed.

St Patrick's in Wapping, also Grade II listed, was established at a similar date and in similar circumstances to St Mary and St Michael's.

St. Paul's, Shadwell.

The present St Paul's Church was designed by John Walters and consecrated in 1820.

A Chapel of Ease, within the Ancient Manor of Stepney, had been built on the site in 1656 by Thomas Neale, a speculative builder, who had developed much of Shadwell.

As the population of Shadwell increased, the inhabitants petitioned for it to be made a parish. This was granted in 1669 and a church was built. The Bishop of London owned the land and the church was to be named after his St Paul's Cathedral. Consecrated in 1671, St Paul's became known as the 'Church of Sea Captains'.

Captain James Cook, the famous explorer, worshipped there and was a Shadwell parishioner. His marriage banns to Elizabeth Batts were read in the church and his son, James, was baptised there in 1763.

Jane Randolph, another parishioner, was baptised in the church in 1720. She married Virginian Peter Jefferson in 1739 and was mother of Thomas Jefferson, the third President of the USA. William Henry Perkin, founder of the modern dyestuff industry, was born in nearby Sutton Street in 1838 and was also baptised in the church.

By 1811 the church was in danger of collapsing and it was closed. With new docks at Poplar and Wapping swelling the population, a petition was made to build a new church. Today's St Paul's was built in 1821 as part of the celebrations to mark the victory at Waterloo.

In the 1840s, the London Dock Company compulsorily purchased half of the churchyard to construct Shadwell New Basin. During the build, it was discovered that the church was slipping into the excavations. Heavy buttressing of the churchyard's retaining wall was needed to save it.

The church survived the Blitz with minor damage.

People's Palace, Mile End Road.

Queen Victoria opened the Queen's Hall of the People's Palace on 16 November 1887. A newspaper at the time called it 'The Albert Hall of East London'. Later, a swimming bath, library, technical school, winter gardens, gymnasium, art school, lecture rooms and rooms for social activities were added. Most of these were paid for by benefactors. The imposing clock tower and drinking fountain were erected in 1890 by Herbert Stern in memory of his father, Baron de Stern.

The idea of a 'Palace of Delight' where the inhabitants of the East End could be provided with culture and education came from a novel by Walter Besant called *All Sorts and Conditions of Men*, a piece of social criticism. The Drapers' Company decided in 1874 to close the Bancroft Almshouses and move Bancroft School to Woodford in Essex. This released land for development and the People's Palace was built on the Bancroft site and became very popular with the public. However, in 1931 a fire destroyed the 3,000 seat Queen's Hall. The magnificent front of the People's Palace survived but the fire cast a shadow over its future. Strong public support led to the building of a new Queen's Hall with a front on Mile End Road. The education part of the complex was separated to become East London College and later in 1934, Queen Mary College, now part of the University of London.

The new People's Palace, an Art Deco building, was opened by King George VI in 1937. Closed during the war for use by local and national governments, it reopened in October 1948 and once again pantomimes, plays, concerts, ballets, variety and films could be enjoyed.

The East End lost another of its landmarks when, because of rising debts, Stepney Borough Council decided it could no longer justify the Palace's costs. It was closed in 1954 and sold to Queen Mary College.

People's Palace, Mile End Road.

Stepney Church.

This is the 'Mother Church of the East End' from which many ecclesiastical institutions and parishes have been derived since the 13th century. It was actually created several centuries earlier as a small wooden construction. Dunstan has been credited with erecting the first stone church on the site of the present one and he dedicated it to All the Saints. As Bishop of London during the 10th century, he would have been Lord of the Manor of Stepney and later became Archbishop of Canterbury. After his canonisation in 1029, the church was dedicated to him and became St Dunstan and All Saints.

The present building, the third on the site, is of Kentish ragstone. It is mainly 15th century and is all in the Perpendicular style, although it retains some interesting traces of an earlier existence as the chancel dates from 200 years earlier. Treasures include one of the few pre-Norman artefacts in London, a 10th century Saxon Rood (cross) under the East window and in the chancel, a 12th century carving of the Annunciation. The East window, showing the risen Christ above the ruins of Stepney after the Blitz, was designed by Hugh Easton.

The church's ten bells were made at the Whitechapel Bell Foundry and were recast in 1806. They are commemorated in the *Oranges and Lemons* nursery rhyme: "... When will that be? Say the bells of Stepney".

The building originally arose in an unpeopled marsh but lay between the old village High Street of Stepney and Whitehorse Street surrounded by its old graveyard. Many victims of the Great Plague of 1665 were buried there.

St Dunstan and All Saints has a long-standing association with the riverside and seafaring. Until recently, births, marriages and deaths at sea were registered at the church which was known as the 'Church of the High Seas'. The Red Ensign flag still flies proudly from its tower, indicating its association with maritime history.

Ratcliff Highway.

This area was immediately outside the Roman settlement of Londinium and led eastwards to Shadwell. A Roman bathhouse was discovered along here during excavations in 2002 and is believed to be connected to buildings excavated in front of Tobacco Dock in the 1970s. The baths were built in the middle of the 3rd century but were dismantled by the 5th. According to Historic England, there were no settlements here until the end of the 16th century, after which it experienced rapid growth following the expansion of the British Empire and riverside trade in Wapping.

Imports of high value goods such as wine, tobacco and animal skins needed secure warehousing and this led to the construction of the London Dock in 1805, which lay to the south of Ratcliff Highway. Sailors from across the world landed at these docks and as the Empire grew so did the notoriety of Ratcliff Highway for being outside what were considered normal rules and morality. This led to a prurient interest by observers and newspapers which reinforced and exaggerated its violent image.

While brothels, lusty foreign sailors and rough trade titivated Victorian society, another sort of trade took place at Jamrach's shop and museum at 179-180 Ratcliff Highway. With thousands of ships arriving and departing annually from the docks, a global trade in wild animals was established by Charles Jamrach who opened his shop here in the 1840s. He became the principal dealer in exotic animals for museums, zoos and wealthy patrons. In 1857 a newly arrived Bengal tiger drew a large crowd to Jamrach's repository store in Betts Street, just north of the Highway. The animal escaped from its crate and grabbed a young boy, who had tried to stroke it, by his neck and ran off. Jamrach chased the tiger and after hitting it with a crowbar rescued the boy. The owner of *Wombwell*'s menagerie read about the incident and bought the tiger for £300.

Jamrach's closed in 1919.

The contemporary photograph shows The Highway in Wapping where Jamrach's once stood.

St George's Library & Town Hall.

The St George-in-the-East Vestry voted to build a library but the one penny on the rates they were allowed to raise would only produce £600. While this was enough to cover the running costs, it was not enough to build the library. So the Vestry asked the public for donations to build the library, with John Passmore Edwards, journalist and philanthropist, providing a substantial amount.

The St George-in-the-East Passmore Edwards Public Library was built next to the Vestry Hall and it opened in 1898, with a children's section added in 1929. The Vestry Hall had been built in 1860. However, through the London Government Act of 1899, the Vestry form of local government was swept away. In its place, metropolitan boroughs were created and with it, Stepney Borough Council. The Council decided to use the Vestry Hall until they could build a new civic home, so in 1900, the building became Stepney Town Hall.

During the Blitz of 1941, the library was bombed and gutted by fire. The shell of the library was left in a highly dangerous state and was pulled down. The site was cleared and remains empty today. A temporary library was built in St George-in-the-East Churchyard with access via Library Place, formally Prospect Place. This library was moved in the late 1980s when a new one was built in Watney Market.

The old Town Hall was neglected after the Council moved out in the 1960s but was used by a variety of Council offices as well as community organisations.

Following recent renovations to the building, St George's Town Hall at 236 Cable Street in Shadwell is now Tower Hamlets Register Office. A Grade II listed building, the magnificent interior still retains much of its former grandeur.

On the west wall of the old Town Hall, on the original library site, is a huge, colourful mural, painted between 1979 and 1983, of scenes from the nearby 'Battle of Cable Street' of 1936.

St. Mary's Shadwell.

This church on Cable Street, Shadwell, consecrated in 1850, was linked to William Quekett, the vicar of Christ Church, Watney Street. Known for his energy and tenacity, William also procured the land where St Peter's London Docks in Wapping was built some years later.

Shadwell in the late 1840s was an area of extreme poverty where the average life expectancy was 27 years. The site where the church now stands was then known as 'no man's land' with tumbledown housing owned by a slum landlord. When Revd. Quekett threatened to expose the landlord in the press, a relative stepped in and, to avoid bad publicity, made some improvements. The site was sold after the death of the landlord but with a portion set aside for a church and the construction of 'model cottages'. These were originally designed by Prince Albert for the 1851 Great Exhibition and built in a number of locations including Cowley Gardens (now Oyster Row). They were north of the railway arches between Lukin and Sutton Street. The film *Sparrows Can't Sing* starring Barbara Windsor was filmed in this location in 1962, just prior to demolition.

Lord Haddo, son of the 4th Earl of Aberdeen who became Prime Minister in 1852, experienced an evangelical conversion in 1848 while living in Brighton. He decided to build a church and paid £800 for the piece of land secured previously by William Quekett in 'no man's land'. Although a man of independent means, he sold paintings and possessions towards the £10,000 needed to build the church. Lord Haddo named it St Mary's in tribute to his wife.

The church's interior was, and remains, very simple. For 80 years there were no stained-glass windows until the 1930s when artist Christopher Powell designed five for the north aisle windows. In 1968 a film starring Laurence Harvey and Mia Farrow called *A Dandy in Aspic* shot some scenes at St Mary's Church.

St. George's Wesleyan Chapel.

The Methodist Chapel on Cable Street, adjacent to what was to become St George's Town Hall, was originally home to middle-class Wesleyan followers. John Wesley was a regular preacher at St George-in-the-East and both he and his brother Charles had preached at meeting houses in Wapping. However, not long after the chapel was built, the population of the surrounding streets soared following the expansion of the docks and railways and this led to the flight of its more affluent residents.

The nature of Methodism—evangelical, anti-alcohol, sermons, Bible studies and being ideologically against popular music and dancing—was not popular in a parish reported to have 154 public houses and brothels and probably as many bawdy music hall songs about press gangs, sailors and thieves.

With its supporters and their money gone, the chapel fell into disrepair. The annual Methodist Conference, where major decisions were made, agreed to pay for the installation of toilets and hot water in 1876 but the chapel remained in debt and deserted. In 1885 the conference agreed that St George's broaden its appeal and become a mission hall. Lancashire-born Peter Thompson, whose name is shown on the postcard, took over the ministry. An account written about him said: "He dreaded the East End for himself and for his wife. The thought of filthy streets and crude humanity filled him with horror and repulsion."

Despite Revd. Thompson's misgivings, he stayed there for 24 years. The mission kept the Cable Street chapel for worship and bought the *Old Mahogany Bar*, now part of *Wilton's Music Hall* and a public house called *Paddy's Goose* in Graces Alley where it set up soup kitchens, second-hand clothing stores and entertainments to attract children.

The 'Wesley-Anns', as they were called in the East End, were, fortunately, in a position to help the local community during the Great Dock Strike of 1889. They provided food for dockworkers and their families as well as places for dockworkers to hold strike meetings.

Interior St. George's Wesleyan Chapel. Cable St. E.

The grand façade of this building, built in 1839, was designed to appeal to tradesmen and more privileged workers. As the pulpit was central to the building for preaching, instead of an altar, there was a Communion table. There was no chancel and no long aisle since processions of the clergy to the altar did not take place. Interior pillars to support the building were deemed acceptable with blank windows. Early morning and watch night (late night) services, love feasts in which the meal recalls the meals Jesus shared with his disciples and Sunday schools were all on the same site.

St George's was rectangular in shape so that the preacher and bible reader could be heard. As it was a place primarily for public worship, it had only one schoolroom and three other rooms. The postcard shows the pulpit in central position with the reader's desk below, and a brass communion rail with cushioned kneelers below the organ pipes. The doors at the bottom led to the other rooms. It also shows the galleries and pews.

At its 1940 Methodist Conference, it was reported that St George's had suffered war damage. By then it was known as St George's Central Hall and had seating for 590 people and chairs instead of pews. The *Old Mahogany Bar* was also damaged but could accommodate 400 people and had seven rooms.

The original building with its imposing façade, portico and steps seems to have been demolished by the late 1950s and a more modest building, known as St George's Methodist Chapel, became a café for teenagers in 1960 and later, a hostel for homeless men, described by the *East London Advertiser* then as 'inadequates'. The chapel was demolished in the 1990s and is now a row of houses called Angel Mews.

London Docks Entrance, Leman Street.

On the corner of East Smithfield and Nightingale Lane (now Thomas More Street) stands the Georgian main gate to the London Docks. Through this gate untold dockworkers and those who worked for the London Dock Company, later the Port of London Authority (PLA), walked to their place of work. Casual dockworkers were 'called on', given a day's work or longer, on the cobblestones just inside the gate.

The London Dock was the second dock built in London and opened in 1805. It was granted a 21-year monopoly on all vessels coming into London laden with wines, brandy and tobacco, except from the West or East Indies. This meant that the London Dock Company had to build huge bonded warehouses and many vaults to store these cargoes. The main architect was Daniel Asher Alexander although much of the work was carried out by John Rennie.

The main gate led to the Western Dock, renamed in the 1850s. The buildings just inside the dock gate were the Company's offices, followed by bonded warehouses running down to the quay area. Below these bonded warehouses were miles and miles of vaults. Here, wines and spirits from all over the world were stored while awaiting delivery to the owner. The dock workers who worked in the vaults were permanent men, employed by the London Dock Company.

In 1969 all this came to an end when the London Docks closed. The heritage-listed bonded warehouses were demolished when News International Printing Works and offices were built in the 1980s. The main gate survives with some alterations. The dock offices are now offices and the roadway is crossed by a large office block.

Rupert Murdoch closed his Wapping print operation in the early 2000s. The buildings were demolished and the valuable land redeveloped into housing, landscaped gardens, shops and offices, called *London Dock*. The new Mulberry Academy London Dock secondary school opened in September 2024.

LONDON DOCKS ENTRANCE, LEMAN STREET.

Interior London Docks. From Wapping Bridge.

Opened in 1805, the Wapping ship entrance was the principal entrance into the London Dock. The entrance led to Wapping Basin and from there into the Dock itself. Over the next 50 years, the London Docks system grew slowly eastward towards Shadwell. To provide access for larger ships then coming into service, a new entrance at Shadwell was built in 1857. Shadwell then became the principal entrance. Consequently, the Wapping entrance was used less and less. By World War Two, it was only used for small craft and barges.

In the 1950s, the Port of London Authority (PLA), the owners of the London Docks, decided to close the Wapping entrance. The swing bridge was removed and a permanent roadway built. The entrance was filled in. However, many of the original entrance features were retained and can still be seen today.

The London Docks itself closed in 1969 and remained derelict until the late 1970s when redevelopment started to take place. A local campaign to save Wapping Basin and the buildings on its eastern side, once used by Harland & Wolff, ship repairers and engineers, was successful. The buildings and Basin became part of what is now called the John Orwell Sports Centre. The Basin was filled in and covered by all-weather pitches for football and hockey and an area for netball and tennis.

The contemporary photograph was taken from the Pier Head looking north.

Interior London Docks from Wapping Bridge.

St. Peter's London Docks

Although consecrated in 1866, the origins of St Peter's Church were laid in 1856 when an Iron Chapel (a pre-fabricated church) was built nearby in Calvert Street and formed part of the St George's Mission. The Iron Chapel could hold 200 people and became so popular that plans were drawn up to build a permanent church and a new parish in Old Gravel Lane, now Wapping Lane.

Father Charles Lowder, the first priest, managed to raise sufficient funds for construction to begin. However, by the time the main parts of the church were complete, funds had run out and the proposed tower and west wing were put on hold. St Peter's Church was built in the fashionable Gothic style with polychromatic brickwork.

In 1881 it was decided to complete the west wing and erect a baptistery and mortuary chapel. A Clergy House was also built on one side of the church entrance and a Sisters House on the other. This created a large archway through which the church is reached.

In 1884, Fr Lincoln Wainright, who had been a curate with Fr Lowder, began his work at St Peter's. He worked without a break for 45 years, providing schools, clubs and medical and nursing facilities for his parishioners. He also served on Stepney Borough Council and was a member of the St George's Board of Guardians. He died in 1929. After his funeral in the church, he was buried in the St Peter's plot at the East London Cemetery, Plaistow.

On 15 October 1940, a bomb fell on the Sisters House killing Sister Elizabeth. The Clergy House was damaged and the interior of the church wrecked. The Blitz also totally destroyed St John of Wapping Church. It was not rebuilt. St Peter's was repaired and in 1951, it was decided to combine the two parishes. Later, St Peter's received a new name: St Peter's, London Docks with St John of Wapping.

St. Peter's London Docks. E.

Since its consecration in 1866, St Peter's has been added to and re-built. Its rich, ornate interior is a reflection of the Anglo-Catholic movement from which it was borne.

This postcard was printed around the 50th anniversary of the founding of St George's Mission to the poor which led to the construction of St Peter's. The interior was subject to much criticism at the time because it resembled a Roman Catholic church. It was described as "of moderate size, with a high-pitched roof and some Gothic pretensions. Its chief features are an east-end rose window containing some very good modern glass and a large metal cross suspended over the chancel steps."

Father Lowder will always be associated with St Peter's. At the beginning, he experienced difficulties but this antagonism soon changed, when during the cholera epidemic of the 1860s, he refused to leave Wapping and worked tirelessly to help the poor and sick. This won the hearts of Wapping people and from then on he became known as 'Father'.

Father's use of incense and lit candles before and during the service was controversial at the time and in 1883 he was accused under the Public Worship Act of having lit candles when not required, wearing illegal vestments, mixing water with wine, using wafers instead of bread, kissing the gospel book and using bells. The case was duly dropped.

After 50 years' work, he died in Austria, where he had gone to recuperate after a long illness. Parishioners raised funds to bring his body home and after a service in a crowded St Peter's, Father was buried in Kent.

Much of St Peter's was damaged in World War Two but new, modern, stained-glass windows, designed by artist Margaret Aldrich Rope, were installed later. More of her work was added to the church in the 1970s following the closure of St Augustine's Church in Haggerston.

St. John's Schools, Wapping

Situated in Church Street (now Scandrett Street), the schools were built in 1760 at the same time as the new St John of Wapping Church, which was built to the left. The original St John of Wapping Church and Churchyard had been built opposite in 1617.

The inscription below the two figures of a boy and girl reads:

> "Erected by Subscription
> AD 1760
> Supported by
> Voluntary Contributions."

There were places for 50 girls and 60 boys.

The schools were in use up to the beginning of World War Two. In 1939 the children were evacuated to the country, safe from enemy bombing. In late 1940, during a heavy raid, incendiary bombs gutted St John of Wapping Church, leaving only the Tower. The schools were also damaged.

After the war, the St John of Wapping Schools did not re-open and the schools were merged with the local St Peter's School. However, part of the schools were lived in after 1945 and steps were taken to convert them into houses. It was not until the 1980s that a serious effort was made to save these historic buildings, which are right in the heart of Wapping, and convert them into living accommodation.

It was at this time that corrugated iron, erected in 1940 in front of the two statues, was removed. To everybody's amazement, the statues had survived the Blitz and had been hidden from the people of Wapping for over 50 years. They can be seen today looking out across the old churchyard, the schools having been converted, finally, into private housing.

St. Johns Schools, Wapping

Children's Hospital. St. George's.

'The Children's Hospital', as it was called locally, in Glamis Road, Shadwell was opened in 1877 by HRH Duchess of Teck.

On their first wedding anniversary, Dr Nathaniel Heckford and his wife, Sarah, moved by the plight of the children along the riverside, had started the original hospital near Ratcliffe Cross Stairs in 1868. With the help of Charles Dickens, who called the hospital 'A Small Star in the East' and wrote about it in *The Uncommercial Traveller*, the Heckfords were able to raise sufficient money to build the 'East London Hospital for Children and Dispensary for Women' in Glamis Road. After purchasing the land for the new hospital, Dr Heckford died a few days later from overwork. He was just 29 years old.

By 1888 the East London Hospital for Children, with 135 beds, was treating 1,003 children in-patients and 18,265 women and children out-patients.

In 1932 the name of the hospital was changed to the 'Princess Elizabeth of York Hospital for Children'. Queen Elizabeth, the Queen Mother's family, the Bowes-Lyons, were large landowners in Shadwell and the road was named after their castle in Scotland.

In 1942, the hospital merged with 'Queen's Hospital for Children' in Hackney Road, Bethnal Green to form the 'Queen Elizabeth Hospital for Children'. Despite the destruction all around, the hospital stayed open throughout World War Two tending the ill, injured and dying.

It was a very sad day for local people when it closed on 30 April 1963 as many of them had been treated at the hospital when children or had had their own children treated there. Within five years the buildings were demolished.

Today the site of the hospital is the Shadwell Community Project's adventure playground for children.

St. George's Church.

St George-in-the-East Church was designed by the famous architect Nicholas Hawksmoor, who was apprenticed to Sir Christopher Wren at around the age of 18. Built between 1714-1729, the Anglican church was consecrated in 1729 and is one of six Hawksmoor churches across London.

The church was badly damaged by enemy bombing and gutted by fire in 1941. The original interior was destroyed by the fire but the walls and distinctive 'pepper-pot' towers stayed up. In the 1950s there was much talk about demolishing the, by then, derelict church, as restoration was seen as too expensive. Thankfully, in the early 1960s, a compromise was reached: the shell of the church was to be retained and a new St George-in-the-East Church built within its historic walls.

This new church has a small courtyard from which its interior can be seen through a splendid glass front. The clock face was removed from the tower and living accommodation incorporated into the wings of the church. A ring of eight replacement bells, cast at the Whitechapel Bell Foundry, was put in place at this time.

The modern, roofless, St George-in-the-East, with its 150 foot-high tower, snow-white Portland stone structure, and still with the scars of war, is a fitting and permanent memorial to all the local Wapping and Shadwell people who experienced suffering and destruction by enemy action during World War Two.

St George-in-the-East Church was designated a Grade I listed building in 1950. It is now on Historic England's *Heritage at Risk Register*.

The contemporary photograph is a view taken from Cannon Street Road.

St. George's Church

St George's Recreation Ground.

Cable Street School can be seen in the background of the postcard. The school, opened in 1898 and built on a former sugar refinery, was big enough for 400 pupils. After World War Two, it became a secondary modern school and the author E. R. Braithwaite taught there, later recording his experiences in his 1959 novel *To Sir, With Love*.

In 1870 the Rector of St George-in-the-East, Revd. Harry Jones campaigned to open both the disused churchyard and the old burial ground of the Wesleyan Chapel to the public. An Act of Parliament in 1852 had closed Church of England burial grounds in London in favour of out-of-town cemeteries. Revd. Jones was passionate about providing some relief to local residents who suffered from the effects of overcrowded housing and the pollution generated by industrial London.

In 1877 the Metropolitan Open Spaces Act was passed and the churchyard was allowed to be opened as a public garden, the site of much of St George's Gardens today. The scheme was recorded in 1883 as being exemplary in its conversion from a burial ground. It had flower beds, seats, a fountain and a public pathway from Cable Street to Ratcliff Highway. A small public mortuary building, built to end poor families keeping the bodies of their dead at home until they could pay for the funeral, closed. In 1904, at a cost of £253 from an anonymous benefactor, the mortuary was converted into a study centre. Many of the exhibits came from ships unloaded by local dockers but they also included a live toad called Tom, beehives, an aviary and a weather station. The study centre was closed during World War Two and never reopened.

The shell of the building still stands. Bricked up and with part of its roof missing, visible above a door are the painted words: 'Metropolitan Borough of Stepney Nature Study Centre'.

The contemporary photograph shows the back of the old school building, now converted into flats.

St. George's Recreation Ground

St. George's Church From Grounds

St George-in-the-East Church is a Grade I listed building. There are many features in its graveyard and grounds that are separately listed as Grade II 'buildings', most notable of which is the Raine Memorial.

Henry Raine was born in 1679 into a wealthy family. As the owner of the *Star Brewhouse* at New Crane Wharf, he made his fortune from brewing. In 1719 Henry founded Raine's Charity Schools in Charles Street (now Raine Street), Wapping. The schools, which provided education for 50 girls and 50 boys, went on to become the Raine's Foundation School. Moving to Arbour Square in Stepney and then Bethnal Green, and after celebrating its tercentenary in St Paul's Cathedral in 2019, Raine's was closed by the London Borough of Tower Hamlets in 2020.

A devout churchman, Henry Raine was a key figure in the creation of the parish of St George-in-the-East in 1729. He married Sarah Petrie from Mile End in 1724 but she died the next year and Henry never re-married. He died in 1738. Both are interred in the Raine family tomb.

The Raine Memorial is in white stone, square on a stepped plinth, surmounted by a truncated spire and enclosed by railings. The texts are to Raine himself, his wife and other relatives, with his coat of arms.

A headstone to Alexander Wyllie, dated 1741, is in buff-coloured sandstone. Above the script-engraved inscription is a bas relief depicting a skull to the left and crossed bones to the right. Other headstones have been relocated against the perimeter walls.

The Marr family, victims of the infamous Ratcliff Highway murderer, were buried in the churchyard.

The War Memorial of 1924 is another feature in the grounds, a slender, tapered white stone shaft with bas relief carvings, sword and leaves on a stepped plinth. There is also the Rectory wall: an 8 foot high, red brick, buttressed wall with white stone coping and the Gate Piers to the church drive.

Wapping Fire Station

In 1865 the Metropolitan Fire Brigade Act established a London-wide emergency fire service and the Metropolitan Fire Brigade (MFB) was formed in 1866. The directly elected London County Council (LCC), formed in 1889, took over the responsibility for MFB operations.

The LCC was keen to illustrate the importance of the modern fire brigade and 1899-1914 saw a period of expansion. A fully motorised fire station opened in 1905 in Red Lion Street (now the corner of Tench Street and Reardon Path). However, it closed in 1920 because the Wapping bridges which let ships pass through the dock system isolated the building.

An inquest into the deaths of three firemen killed by a fire at Lower Oliver's Wharf recorded their deaths as accidental. A Fire Brigade Committee report claimed that the closure of Wapping Fire Station in 1920 had no bearing on their deaths.

Surviving demolition, the building has had a varied history since its closure.

Hit by an incendiary bomb, the firemen's quarters were quickly converted into flats to rehouse people made homeless by the Blitz.

The ground floor became the National Dock Labour Board office for Wapping after nationalisation. Better known as the office for 'bomping on', it was where dockers would wait for work. If there was none, they pushed their registration books through the window or 'box' to be stamped for a subsistence payment.

By 1957, the old fire station had become Wapping Boys' Club and part of a network, under the patronage of the Duke of Edinburgh, offering sports and pastimes. In 1959, Pathé News filmed the Duke in Wapping where the boys were seen playing snooker, chess and draughts.

By the mid-1960s the building was derelict again and there were plans for it to be taken over by a local greengrocer, Bill Leonard. Come 1969 it was a youth club once more and remains so today. A stone inscription on the front commemorates its opening on 21 December 1905.

Wapping Fire Station

Wapping Bridge, Showing Wapping Church

The swing bridge on Wapping High Street went over the principal entrance into the London Dock. Opened in 1805, the London Dock was built in the days of sail. However, the entrance, soon after its completion, could not handle the bigger ships coming into service. This led to the London Dock Company building a larger entrance at Shadwell. Slowly the use of this new entrance reduced the amount of shipping using the Wapping entrance until it mainly handled small vessels and barges.

In the 1950s, the swing bridge was removed and a permanent road constructed. The entrance was filled in and landscaped.

St John of Wapping Church was built in 1760, replacing one built in 1617 in the churchyard.

In December 1940, St John suffered a direct hit by incendiary bombs and was gutted. Only the Tower, badly damaged, and the outer walls remained. The congregation was merged with nearby St Peter's, London Docks Church. The Tower was restored by the London County Council after the war.

The shell of St John survived until the 1990s when it was incorporated into flats built on the site in the shape of the old church. These residences are on the corner of Green Bank and Scandrett Street.

The contemporary photograph shows the junction of Vaughan Way with Knighten Street, the approximate location of the Fielding image.

Wapping Bridge, Showing Wapping Church

Tunnel Pier, L.C.C.

Tunnel Pier was one of the stopping points on the London County Council's Steamboat Service. Starting on 17 June 1905, 'The Penny Steamers', its nickname at the time, had 30 paddle boats on the run from Hammersmith to Greenwich. However, despite carrying over ten million passengers in the three years of its existence, the Steamboat Service was declared uneconomic and was closed.

Tunnel Pier was named after the nearby Thames Tunnel built by father and son Brunel between 1825 and 1843. Also nearby is King Henry's Wharf, the site of Execution Dock, where pirates and smugglers were hanged and their bodies left to be washed over by three tides.

Tunnel Pier was later administered by the Port of London Authority. W.H.J. Alexander, whose headquarters and repair yard were a little way up river, used the Pier to moor his famous *Sun* tugs while they were being repaired.

The Pier also played an important part in the lives of Wapping people during World War Two. During the famous air raid on 7 September 1940—the beginning of the Blitz—Wapping was alight from one end to the other. Because all the bridges were open, a standing order during an air raid, Wapping became an island. The people of Wapping had to be evacuated by water. A fleet of river craft was assembled and people were evacuated upstream to safety. In fact, some were taken as far as Richmond, over ten miles to the west.

The Pier is now owned by Woods River Cruises Ltd who run a fleet of all kinds of vessels on the River Thames.

The contemporary photograph shows the Pier view from King Henry's Stairs.

The Sailors' Home, Well Street, & Dock Street, London Docks. Founded 1830.

The Sailors' Home has its origins in the collapse of the Royal Brunswick Theatre in Well Street (now Ensign Street) on 28 February 1828. The Revd. George Smith, minister at the Methodist Mariners Church in Wellclose Square, heard the crash and ran to the disaster scene, organising the rescue of the injured and recovery of bodies. While amongst the rubble, he was seized by a vision: the theatre collapse was an act of God and a sign that he should build a sailors' home on the site. A home, he argued, would save the seafarer from the crimping system and would offer seamen protection from this by providing secure accommodation, good food, a chapel, a bank to deposit their pay in and a haven against alcohol.

In 1830 the Sailors' Home was founded and it opened in 1835 with lodging for 100 seafarers, expanding later to 500. The internal design of the home, whose main entrance then was on Well Street, was similar to a prison. Sailors had individual metal cages arranged around a central open square. This was the first modern home for sailors and it became the model and name for similar establishments worldwide.

In the late 1870s an extension was built that fronted Dock Street, becoming its main entrance. In 1893 the London School of Nautical Cookery opened at the Sailors' Home to train ships' cooks. The London Nautical School was also set up at the same time.

In 1955, the building fronting Dock Street was demolished and a new one built with better facilities. To reflect changing times, the Sailors' Home was given a modern name—the *Red Ensign Club*. The 1960s saw the demise of the British Merchant Fleet and with it the need for fewer seamen. The *Red Ensign Club* closed on New Year's Eve 1974.

The two buildings on Dock Street and Ensign Street remain and are now used as a hostel called *Wombat's* for backpackers and business travellers alike.

Pier Head. Wapping

The houses at Wapping Pier Head, facing each other across the original lock entrance to the London Dock, are the finest Georgian riverside domestic dwellings in the Docklands. Not surprisingly, they are very desirable residences. They were built for officials of the London Dock Company between 1811 and 1813 to the designs of Daniel Asher Alexander.

The lock entrance was designed by the famous engineer John Rennie in 1805. By the 1930s the original locks of the London Docks became far too small for the ocean-going ships of the day. Only those ships that were engaged in coastal and continental trades entered the docks.

The London Docks became a vast storehouse for a variety of different cargoes. Wool, stored in many of the warehouses, occupied nearly one million square feet of space. Other goods included rubber, tobacco, spices, ivory, alcohol, tea and coffee.

The Wapping entrance lock was filled in during the 1960s and by the late 1980s the whole of the London Docks system had been transformed into houses and flats.

Wapping Old Stairs are found beside the *Town of Ramsgate* public house, a small riverside tavern taking its name from small packets and fishing boats from Ramsgate that used to moor beside the Stairs. It is reputed that the infamous 'hanging' Judge Jeffreys was caught at Wapping Old Stairs trying to flee to France after the abdication of James II.

The contemporary photograph shows landscaping for Pier Head residents, with Oliver's Wharf and the Metropolitan Police's Marine Policing Unit workshop in the distance.

The Jetty London Docks

The London Dock Company had a Parliamentary Act passed in 1800 giving it permission to build an enclosed dock at Wapping.

Construction began in 1802 when the foundation stone was laid by Prime Minister Henry Addington. The London Dock was opened in 1805. Built in the days of sail, the London Dock could handle a few hundred vessels. The success of the London Dock was down to its proximity to the City of London and its merchants and the valuable goods it landed — wool, brandy, wine and spices.

Despite the opening of Tobacco Dock and the Eastern Dock, new warehouse space and a quay area were needed in the London Dock itself, which was now renamed the Western Dock. So, in 1831, a central Jetty was constructed into the middle of the Western Dock. This gave increased quay space and allowed the construction of more warehouse facilities on the Jetty itself. In the 1920s, the Jetty was made more substantial with the use of reinforced concrete.

The Jetty was demolished in the 1970s together with the wholesale destruction of most of the London Docks and their vaults and warehouses.

News International Printing Works — known locally as Fortress Wapping — was constructed in the 1980s on the site of the historic vaults and warehouses, while a housing development covered the Jetty site (Kennet Street and Waterman Way). Later, the News International site became vacant and was demolished to make way for the development of the new *London Dock* complex of housing, shops and a new school.

The contemporary photograph shows Waterman Way houses fronting the ornamental canal.

Dockers' Cottages. Pennington St. E

These cottages were terraced houses that ran along Pennington Street and streets running off Ratcliff Highway to Pennington Street. Three of them — Chigwell, Artichoke and Breezer's Hill — still remain. Although John's Hill where this photograph was taken no longer exists, it provides a window into another time.

Charles Booth in his walks around the area with Police Inspectors Drew and Reid recorded that there were many brothels in this street: "Cockney, Irish and some thieves, a good number of prostitutes, but of a sturdy kind and there are no bullies (pimps). It is not like the west end." While the children in Pennington Court were described as "booted, well fed and clean", John's Hill, however, was "much trouble to police. The windows were broken, pitch and toss going on. German Prostitutes".

Booth continues, noting that further along the street towards Chigwell Hill, lived some respectable men who were City Police and dock labourers in a dock company building. At Lavender Place, a little further east, the children were clean and booted and the houses had windows. In the postcard some of the windows appear to be broken (although this could just have been reflections). Nevertheless, the children are well dressed and booted. It may be that the postcard, which was printed just a few years after Booth's final volume was published in 1903, was an act of defiance against the establishment and its vicarious interest in sensationalising poverty.

By 1936 much of the terrace was derelict or already demolished. Aerial photographs taken on 18 May 1948 show four bomb sites between Pennington Street and The Highway. A documentary film made by Humphrey Jennings in 1943 called *Fires Were Started* show firemen in Pennington Street putting out fires close to the location of these cottages.

John's Hill was between Artichoke Hill and Chigwell Hill, an area currently occupied by light industrial buildings and a new housing development.

Whitechapel Library & Art Gallery.

The Whitechapel Library was founded by the Victorian philanthropist John Passmore Edwards and opened in 1891. Its nickname was 'the university of the Ghetto' being at the hub of the Jewish East End and providing an education for notable names such as Jacob Bronowski, Arnold Wesker and Isaac Rosenberg. A blue plaque for Isaac can be found at the old library entrance.

Thousands of local people packed the reading rooms, hungry for knowledge from the newspapers and books they lacked in their own homes. The library became synonymous with local history and its working-class struggles and yearnings, representing an ideal of self-improvement.

Surviving the Blitz, the library finally closed in August 2005. Its place in the community has been superseded by the Idea Store Whitechapel.

The Whitechapel Art Gallery was built in 1898 next to the Whitechapel Library in Whitechapel High Street and was opened by Lord Rosebery in March 1901. Designed by Charles Harrison Townsend, the impressive narrow-fronted building, clad in terracotta tiles, is fairly small but gives the appearance of being much bigger.

An art gallery in the East End was the dream of Revd. Canon Samuel Barnett of St Jude's Church in Commercial Street, and his wife, Henrietta. In the 1880s, he started to bring art to local people by staging exhibitions in a local school. He believed that art "would educate people so that they might realise the extent and the meaning of the past, the beauty of nature and the substance of hope". Then in 1899, he started a charity to raise money to build a permanent art gallery.

Over the years, artists, thinkers, writers and academics both locally and from across the globe have come to the gallery and helped to enrich the cultural offer of its neighbourhood with bold, often radical exhibitions and educational activities. In 2009, the gallery expanded its space into the adjacent former library building.

Stepney Temple. Commercial Rd. E.

The Wesleyans reached out to the many sailors in the area and formed the Wesleyan Methodist Seaman's Mission in 1843. In 1889, the St George's East End Mission work expanded when they took over the Seamen's Chapel in Commercial Road, renaming it the 'Stepney Temple'.

With his eye to the future, the Revd. Peter Thompson planned that when the lease for the Temple expired in 1906 (the date of the postcard) and also those of the surrounding properties, he would acquire the leases on all those buildings. To this end, they were able to build new premises and reinvent it as the Stepney Central Hall with seating for 2,000 people. School rooms, a medical mission and accommodation for workers were also created as well as shops that fronted onto Commercial Road which were let out for £500 a year. Films were shown which cost one halfpenny for admission—the 'penny pictures'. These attracted 2,000 children for the early show and the same number of adults in the evening.

Stepney Central Hall received a direct hit during the Blitz, destroying most of it. Not everyone was happy to see Stepney Temple demolished. A local newspaper said that the stately frontage had been a feature of the building since the early 19th century and a landmark along that part of Commercial Road.

The noticeboards in the postcard are advertising the 22nd anniversary of the Methodists' East End Mission with speeches by the Revd. Thompson.

Football commentator John Motson lived at the mission in the 1960s while his father was a minister there.

Just over a century after it was built in 1907, the Central Hall was demolished to make way for a block of residential flats, now called Marlin Apartments, with just the front of the hall remaining.

Swedish Lutheran Church Princess Square.

The Swedish Lutheran Church in Prince's Square was built in the Parish of St George-in-the-East in 1729 and was the first Swedish church in Britain.

It was said the Scandinavians warmed their hands on the Great Fire of London in 1666; importing timber for the rebuilding made them rich. Most of the timber was landed at Wapping, Shadwell, Ratcliff and Limehouse.

The plainness of the Swedish church reflected the strict Lutheran religion. It was small with galleries to accommodate as many as possible including members of the Swedish Embassy. The Swedish scientist Emanuel Swedenborg had been living in London. He died in 1772 and was buried in the church vaults. Also buried there was the Swedish botanist, Dr Daniel Solander, who had sailed in *HMS Endeavour* with Captain James Cook.

By the second half of the 19th century, the timber trade had moved to Surrey Docks and with it, the Scandinavians. The church went into decline. When news about its demolition reached the Swedish government, Emanuel's remains were returned to Sweden and reburied in Uppsala Cathedral.

The Swedish Lutheran Church was demolished in 1921 and Prince's Square was renamed Swedenborg Square and made into a children's playground. This area was badly damaged during the Blitz and in the 1960s, the London County Council decided to clear the site and build St George's Estate. This act of wanton vandalism destroyed some of the architectural gems of Stepney. Parts of the estate were named Swedenborg Gardens, Stockholm House and Solander Gardens.

A small baptismal font from the Swedish church was dedicated on 18 June 1960 to commemorate the site of the church within the new estate.

The contemporary photograph is a view of Swedenborg Gardens taken from the playground.

Index of Postcard Captions by Topic

London Docks

Interior London Docks. From Wapping Bridge 40

London Docks Entrance, Leman Street 38

Pier Head. Wapping 64

The Jetty, London Docks 66

Tunnel Pier, L.C.C. 60

Wapping Bridge, Showing Wapping Church 58

Municipal Buildings

Children's Hospital. St George's 48

People's Palace, Mile End Road 24

St George's Library & Town Hall 30

The Sailors' Home, Well Street & Dock Street, London Docks. Founded 1830 62

Wapping Fire Station 56

Whitechapel Library & Art Gallery 70

Streets/Shops/Schools

Dockers' Cottages. Pennington St. E. 68

Ratcliff Highway 28

St John's Schools, Wapping 46

Watney Market, Commercial Road End 12

Watney Street E. (C.A. Fielding shop) 8, 10

Religious Buildings

Christ Church (interior). Watney St. 16

Christ Church, Watney Street 14

Interior St. George's Wesleyan Chapel, Cable St. E. 36

Stepney Church (St. Dunstan's) 26

Stepney Temple. Commercial Rd. E. 72

St. George's Church 50

St. George's Church From Grounds 54

St. George's Recreation Ground 52

St. George's Wesleyan Chapel 34

St. Mary's Shadwell 32

St. Mary's & St. Michael's Church. Commercial Rd. E. 18

St. Mary's & St. Michael's Church (interior) Commercial Road. E. 20

St. Paul's Shadwell 22

St. Peter's London Docks 42

St. Peter's London Docks. E. (interior) 44

Swedish Lutheran Church Princess Square 74

About the Author

Ray Newton was born in Shadwell, East London and lived there all his life. He died at home aged 86. Living not far from the Tower of London, he was a fountain of knowledge on the history of Shadwell, Wapping and surrounding areas, sharing this and his insights through walks, talks and publications. Ray could trace his family in Shadwell back to at least 1820.

Ray became a lecturer in social sciences and later local history and through the latter, met Madge Darby, an historian who lived in Wapping. Together, they set up the History of Wapping Trust in 1984. Trustees of the charity continue their legacy today to promote the history of Wapping and Shadwell. Ray was firstly the Secretary and then, Chairman, of the Trust. A keen gardener, Ray tended to his fruit and vegetables at the Cable Street Community Gardens up until his death.

After he had started to collaborate with Steve Kentfield to buy and sell postcards at markets and fairs in the UK, Ray recognised their value in adding to his local history lectures and walks. Soon Ray held a large collection of pictorial East End postcards which included those of Fielding.

Ray was born in 1938, one of three boys and a girl born to his father, Thomas, and mother, Emma. After National Service, and at the age of 23, Ray took over from his father as the publican of *The Cock*, opposite Free Trade Wharf on The Highway. The public house was later demolished to make way for the widening of The Highway. Moving on to work for his elder brother in his betting shops, Ray decided at 32 to get an education. He studied for 'O' and 'A' Levels at evening classes and then took a Social Sciences degree course at Middlesex Polytechnic. He became a lecturer in social sciences at West Ham College and also taught local history at Adult Education classes in the Shadwell Institute, now the Shadwell Centre within Tower Hamlets. Ray's local history walks and talks and postcard fairs usually ended up in a pub over a few pints with friends. Wetherspoons will surely be missing his custom. Ray was a lifelong Millwall supporter.

One tradition that will be missed is the annual distribution of Ray's homemade Christmas puddings, made exclusively for family and a few select friends. He worked as a chef for the Officers' Mess during his National Service in the Army and continued to enjoy cooking. He made the puddings with military precision.

Fielding Postcards is Ray's third publication for the History of Wapping Trust after *A Riverside Journey* (1990) and *South of Commercial Road* (2001).

Ray never married but is survived by his younger sister, Sylvie, and numerous nieces and nephews, who enjoyed many happy holidays and adventures with Uncle Ray.

Raymond Victor Newton, born 3 March 1938, died 30 April 2024

Our Production Process

Ray Newton from the History of Wapping Trust, Steve Kentfield with his website of East London postcards and Phil Mernick from the East London History Society all provided access to original Fielding postcards in their private collections. Thirty-three unique postcards were found amongst these three collections and it is thought that this is the total number published by Fielding.

For over 20 years, Ray wrote a monthly article on the history of a particular postcard called *Postcard of the Month* and this was published on Steve's *The East London Post Card Site*. Ray lived in Shadwell all his life and his knowledge of Wapping, Shadwell and the immediate areas was immense. At the time of his death in April 2024, Ray had already written the history on most of the Fielding postcards published here and this forms the bulk of the 'then' information. Research and writing of new text have been undertaken by Amanda Day and Helen Keep to fill the gaps left by Ray on the historical content of the remaining postcards. The style of writing, therefore, will differ slightly. All information, however, has been brought up to the present day (2025) to reflect the 'now' situation and this is accompanied by a contemporary photograph taken in 2024/25 by John Tarby.

Many of the postcards were owned by all three collectors. Nevertheless, we photographed every one and this duplication enabled us to choose the best example for our book.

All the postcards originate from black and white photographs and are believed to be printed by the photochrome lithographic process on textured paper. This created two problems. The slightly rough surface is recorded when copied in a scanner and photographing them produces a similar effect which is not wanted. Also, the dot structure from litho printing can create interference (Moiré) patterns in the photographs.

The original postcards were photographed on a copy stand using a Leica M10P camera with a 55mm Micro Nikkor, a favourite lens for this type of work. Special lighting was used to eliminate the paper texture in the photographs, leaving only the printed image in their reproduction. Interference patterns were reduced with image software. The locations for the contemporary photographs were found using various Old Ordnance Survey Maps by *The Godfrey Edition*.

The subjects of the 33 postcards fall into four topic areas: London Docks, Municipal Buildings, Religious Buildings and Streets/Shops/Schools. Half of the collection covers Religious Buildings. Geographically, they show Wapping, Shadwell, Whitechapel and Mile End. An index is available for the reader to identify specific places or buildings under each topic.

The postcard captions have been reproduced as they were published by Fielding, complete with punctuation and in some cases, factual errors. The facts have been corrected in our historical text.

We have debated what is the reasoning behind Charles Fielding's choice of subjects in his postcards. Most are grand buildings but then we see the Pennington Street view showing poverty. Is it just 'seize the moment' photography? Our research in libraries has often highlighted the fact that, to the best of our knowledge, some Fielding postcards are the only image of a building or scene that no longer exists, for example Stepney Temple and St George's Wesleyan Chapel.

Our Other Publications

Waeppa's People — A History of Wapping by Madge Darby
A5, softback, 90pp, illustrated, £3.50 (out of print)
Pub. 1988 by Conner & Butler, ISBN 0 947699

William Peckover of Wapping — Gunner of the Bounty by Madge Darby
A5, softback, illustrated, maps, 14pp, £1.00
Pub. 1989 by Conner & Butler, ISBN 0 947699 12 0

Judge Jeffreys and the Ivy Case by Madge Darby
A5, softback, illustrated, maps, 42pp, £3.00
Pub. 1989 by Conner & Butler, ISBN 0 947699 13 9

Colonel Thomas Rainsborough — Wapping's Most Famous Soldier (1610-1648) by Lincoln S. Jones
A5, softback, illustrated, map, 18pp, £1.20
Pub. 1990 by History of Wapping Trust, ISBN 1 873086 03 2

The Hermitage Shelter Minutes — December 1940 (An air raid shelter in Hermitage Wharf) by Madge Darby
A5, softback, illustrated, map, 18pp, £1.20
Pub. 1990 by History of Wapping Trust, ISBN 1 873086 01 6

A Riverside Journey — In Picture Postcards by Steve Kentfield, Ray Newton
A4, softback, 54pp, £4.95
Pub. 1990 by History of Wapping Trust, ISBN 1 873086 02 4

South of Commercial Road — A Photographic Record 1934-1997 by R.Newton, J.Tarby, S.Kentfield, T.Newton
A4, softback, 44pp, £5.95
Pub. 2001 by History of Wapping Trust, ISBN 1 873086 04 0

Piety and Piracy — The History of Wapping and St Katharine's by Madge Darby
Royal Octavo perfect bound, 96pp, £9.95
Pub. 2011 by History of Wapping Trust, ISBN 978–1 873086 06 3

Captain Bligh in Wapping 1785-1790 by Madge Darby
Royal Octavo perfect bound, 60pp, £7.50
Pub. 2017 by History of Wapping Trust, ISBN 9781 873086 07 0

Wapping on VE Day — Commemorating 80 years
A5, booklet, 20pp, £5.00
Pub. 2025 by History of Wapping Trust

Fielding Postcards presents a unique set of 33 colour picture postcards celebrating the East End of London, together with a brief history of each scene and a contemporary photograph. These postcards have been drawn from the private collections of three passionate collectors, including local historian, Ray Newton.

Hidden from general view until now, the postcards reveal what life was like in the early 1900s, particularly in Wapping and Shadwell, with scenes showing docks, streets, churches and important municipal buildings.

This book documents the postcard output of Charles Fielding, an enterprising newsagent turned postcard publisher, in Watney Street. With a very distinctive and recognisable style amongst postcard collectors, Fielding is considered to be the only publisher of postcards of the 'Golden Age' working in Shadwell.

Through his colourful images, Fielding provides an alluring glimpse of the East End with scenes that remain as captivating now as they were at the height of the Edwardian postcard collecting craze.

Fielding Postcards complements our first book of postcards—*A Riverside Journey*.

ISBN 978-1-873086-08-7

£14.95

Published by
History of Wapping Trust
Charity Reg. No. 290087

9 781873 086087

Colour scenes from the early 1900s of London's East End published by newsagent Charles Fielding